Great Journeys

The Search for the Northwest Passage

Jill Foran

WEIGL PUBLISHERS INC.

Published by Weigl Publishers Inc.
350 5th Avenue, Suite 3304, PMB 6G
New York, NY 10118-0069

Web site: www.weigl.com

Library of Congress Cataloging-in-Publication Data
Foran, Jill.
  The search for the Northwest Passage / Jill Foran.
      p. cm. -- (Great journeys)
  Includes index.
  ISBN 1-59036-205-5 (library binding : alk. paper) — ISBN 1-59036-259-4 (pbk.)
  1. Northwest Passage--Discovery and exploration--Juvenile literature. 2. Arctic regions--Discovery and exploration--Juvenile literature. I. Title. II. Great journeys (Weigl Publishers)
  G640.F67 2005
  910'.9163'27--dc22

2004002875
Printed in the United States of America
3 4 5 6 7 8 9 0   12 11 10 09 08

Project Coordinator
Donald Wells
Substantive Editor
Tina Schwartzenberger
Copy Editor
Janice L. Redlin
Photo Researcher
Andrea Harvey
Design & Layout
Bryan Pezzi

Credits
Every reasonable effort has been made to trace ownership and to obtain permission to reprint copyright material. The publishers would be pleased to have any errors or omissions brought to their attention so that they may be corrected in subsequent printings.

Cover: Arctic icebergs (Photos.com); **Daryl Benson/Masterfile:** page 7; **Corel Corporation:** pages 3, 5T, 5B, 16, 17L, 26; **John Foster/Masterfile:** page 25; **Glenbow Archives:** pages 18 (NA-694-1), 19 (NA-1512-1), 29 (NA-694-1; NA-1512-1); **Bryan Pezzi:** pages 12, 13; **Photos.com:** pages 1, 4, 6, 8, 10, 11, 14, 15, 17R, 21, 22, 23L, 23R, 24, 27R, 29; **James P. Rowan:** page 20; **Galen Rowell/CORBIS/MAGMA:** page 9; **Jim Steinhart:** page 27L.

On the Cover: Icebergs are a hazard to ships sailing through the Northwest Passage.

Contents

The Long Search

The Northwest Passage is a sea route. It links the Atlantic and Pacific oceans. It runs through Canada's maze of Arctic islands. The passage lies between Canada and Greenland. It is about 500 miles (805 kilometers) north of the Arctic Circle and only 1,200 miles (1,931 km) from the North Pole. It is a difficult route. It is plagued by countless icebergs, biting winds, and freezing temperatures. These conditions prevented European explorers from discovering the existence of the Northwest Passage until well into the nineteenth century.

In the late fifteenth century, it was believed that a northern passage would provide a new shipping route from Europe to Asia. For the next four centuries, bold explorers set out to find and complete this passage. They struggled through the **labyrinth** of Arctic islands and channels. They failed, time and again, to find a northwest passage. Despite all the failed **expeditions** and tragedies, many explorers did not give up in their search. They faced starvation and disease to find the mysterious passage. Sadly, many of them died in their quest.

The existence of a northwest passage was proved in the 1850s by Robert McClure. It was many years, however, before anyone was able to sail the entire passage. This journey was first completed between 1903 and 1906 by the Norwegian explorer Roald Amundsen.

Fascinating Fact
It is known today that there is more than one Northwest Passage. The melting and shifting ice in the Arctic regularly creates or blocks passages.

Navigational equipment such as this antique compass helped early explorers search for the Northwest Passage.

The Unforgiving North

Wildlife and extreme weather conditions are some obstacles that northern explorers must overcome.

Early explorers to the Arctic discovered a harsh environment. The Arctic was filled with icebergs, brutal winds, narrow straits, winding channels, and many islands. The biggest challenge was the ice. Explorers soon learned that the sea in the far North froze over for most of the year. Sometimes the ice trapped the explorers' ships. In some cases, it crushed ships. The luckier expeditions waited out the winter and continued exploring after the ice melted. Winters in the Arctic are dark and frigid. Temperatures often fall to -50° Fahrenheit (-46° Celsius). The winds never cease. The Sun barely shines. Early explorers trapped in the Arctic during the winter usually suffered greatly.

Winter temperatures average -27.4° Fahrenheit (-33° Celsius) in the Arctic.

The desire for wealth and riches inspired the search for the Northwest Passage. Italian explorer John Cabot knew that England wanted to find a new sea route that would lead to China's gold, silk, and spices. The eastern routes around Africa to Asia were long and difficult. Worse, they were blocked by Spanish or Portuguese warships. In the late 1490s, Cabot convinced King Henry VII of England to pay for an expedition to the northern regions of the Americas. Cabot knew the world was bigger than Christopher Columbus claimed. He told King Henry that Columbus had not sailed far enough to reach Asia. He believed he could find a shorter, more direct passage to Asia across the top of North America.

Cabot did not find the route to Asia. However, the idea of a Northwest Passage to easy riches persisted. Beginning in the early sixteenth century, many European countries sent explorers to find this direct passage to Asia. As they searched for this route, early explorers managed to map much of North America. However, they could not find the fabled Northwest Passage. The search for a northern shipping route was not abandoned. In 1745, the British House of Commons offered a £20,000 reward—millions of dollars in today's money—to whoever found the passage.

Fascinating Fact
Pepper was more valuable than gold in eleventh-century Europe.

The Riches of Cathay

In the early days of exploration, Europeans called China "Cathay." This was a medieval name. It was made popular in the 1300s by the writings of Italian explorer Marco Polo. For centuries, Europeans read stories and descriptions of Cathay. Many of these writings described the wealth of this mysterious country. From these stories, Europeans came to believe that Cathay was a land of untold riches. Therefore, the desire to gain access to this wealth and establish trade with Cathay and other parts of Asia was strong. In the fifteenth century, the southern routes to Asia were mapped and controlled by Spain and Portugal. By the early 1500s, both countries were bringing back riches, such as pepper, through these southern routes.

The Chinese junk is one of the strongest, most seaworthy ships ever built.

Ship Shape

With the exception of a few **overland** treks, the search for the Northwest Passage took place in ships. Over the course of 400 years, the style and size of these ships varied greatly. In the early years of the quest, explorers used whatever ship was available and affordable. Many of these ships were considered **sophisticated** for their time. They often were not suitable for the harsh, ice-laden waters of the North. Still, many of these ships managed to withstand the harsh environment and heavy beating of the North Atlantic waves for more than one journey. In the 1600s, the sturdy 55-ton (50-metric tonne) *Discovery* was used for six voyages to the North.

Fascinating Fact
By the nineteenth century, some of the larger ships sent to the Arctic were equipped with libraries for the crew.

Gradually, ships sent to the North became more powerful and reliable. Wooden ships were strengthened to make them seaworthy for Arctic sailing. **Hulls** were reinforced with a second layer of oak planking. The **bows** of the vessels were **sheathed** in metal. This helped them butt their way through sheet ice. For example, the Norwegian ship *Fram*—which means "forward" in Norwegian—was built in 1892 to withstand Arctic ice. The *Fram* had a triple oak/greenwood hull that was 24 to 28 inches (61–71 centimeters) thick. It could proceed under steam or sail power. The *Fram* was so sturdy it was able to make two trips to the Arctic and one trip to the Antarctic.

Samuel Hearne was the first European to walk from Hudson Bay to the Arctic Ocean.

Early explorers did not have the luxury of using radio, radar, and computers to calculate the position of their ships. Among the early **navigation** tools used by Arctic explorers were the cross-staff and the back-staff. The cross-staff was first used in the early 1400s to determine a ship's latitude, or position north or south of the equator. First, a sailor would use the cross-staff to find the **altitude** of the stars, Moon, or Sun. From this measurement, navigators could find their ship's latitude. In the late 1500s, English explorer John Davis (also spelled Davys) invented the back-staff to determine a ship's latitude. Davis's back-staff was a welcome invention because it allowed sailors to stand with their backs to the Sun while taking measurements.

Enormous ice-breaking ships help explorers reach uncharted areas of the Arctic.

9

Hopeless Race to Riches

Beginning in the sixteenth century, several European countries were anxious to find a northern passage to Asia. These countries included France, England, and Holland. In the 1520s and 1530s, France sent explorers such as Giovanni de Verrazano and Jacques Cartier to find a route to Asia through North America. In the early 1600s, Holland's Dutch East India Company sponsored expeditions to find a northern passage on behalf of Dutch merchants. Everyone wanted to have control over this passage.

The English were the most persistent explorers in search of the Northwest Passage. In the 1570s, England sent Martin Frobisher and John Davis to the Far North on different expeditions. These two men managed to explore as far as Baffin Bay and the Davis Strait. In the 1610s and 1620s, there were more efforts by English explorers. These expeditions were frustrating. Early explorers encountered blocked channels, dead ends, and freezing weather. They learned that the Arctic had a harsh environment that was difficult for Europeans to endure. These voyages proved to England and other countries that the Northwest Passage through the Arctic might exist. However, it would not be an easy or fast trade route. Hopes for an easy trade route across the top of North America to Asian riches faded.

Fascinating Fact
While many explorers were searching for the Northwest Passage, others searched for the Northeast Passage to Asia. The Northeast Passage was thought to run north of Scandinavia, into the Arctic Basin, and along the north coast of Asia.

The British East Indies Company was formed in 1600 to conduct trade in Asia. The company ruled India from the mid-1700s to 1858.

The Merchant Adventurers

England's merchants played a large role in initiating early expeditions to the North. English merchants wanted to find foreign markets for their goods, especially their cloth. They believed that one of the best markets for their goods would be in Asia. In December 1553, a group of London merchants formed the Merchant Adventurers, or the Company of Merchant Adventurers of England for the Discovery of Lands Unknown. This company was established to pay for voyages of exploration. The Merchant Adventurers raised enough money to buy and equip three ships. These ships were to be used for a voyage to Asia. The Merchant Adventurers decided to attempt a northeast route to Asia instead of a northwest route. Their expedition failed to reach Asia.

In recent years, large pieces of Arctic ice have broken apart and started to melt. Less ice may make it easier to travel through the Northwest Passage.

Arctic Maps

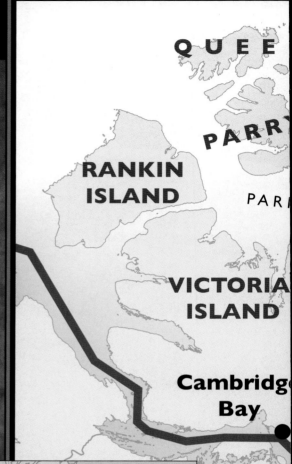

Some scientists think that **global warming** will open the Northwest Passage to cruise ships, tankers, and warships within 50 years. The route through the Northwest Passage from Europe to the Far East is 2,485 miles (4,000 km) shorter than the route through the Panama Canal. Some people have started to refer to the Northwest Passage as the Panama Canal North.

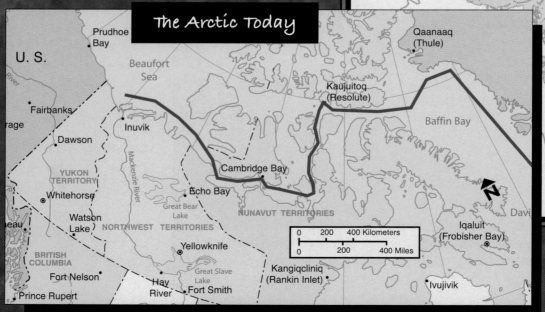

The Arctic Today

12

LIZABETH ISLANDS

ISLANDS

GREENLAND

HANNEL

Resolute

BAFFIN BAY

BAFFIN ISLAND

Gjoa Harbour

| 0 | 100 | 200 Kilometers |
| 0 | 100 | 200 Miles |

Roald Amundsen's Voyage
1903 to 1906

Unexpected Encounters

Europeans were not the first people to explore the Arctic. The Inuit had lived in the vast region for more than 1,000 years before the arrival of European explorers. The Inuit were **nomadic** people who had learned to survive in one of the coldest places on Earth. Until the sixteenth century, they had no contact with Europeans. They knew little about the world beyond their region. Similarly, early explorers knew nothing about the Inuit. However, over the next few hundred years, many northern explorers and groups of Inuit encountered one another.

Sometimes these encounters were filled with violence and tragedy. The Europeans and the Inuit did not always know what to expect from each other. This could lead to disagreements or battles. One such battle occurred in 1612. That year, explorer Thomas Button and his men tried to **commandeer** canoes from some Inuit. A fight broke out. Five of Button's men were killed.

Friendships also developed between the Inuit and the explorers. In 1585, John Davis and his crew made friends with several Inuit. They entertained the Inuit with music and gave them gifts. Other European explorers had similar experiences. The Inuit supplied explorers with valuable information about the uncharted coast. They also showed the Europeans how to stay alive in the harsh environment. The Inuit taught European explorers how to hunt for caribou, fish for seals, and prevent frostbite.

The Inuit wore masks as a way of praying that there were many animals to hunt.

Inukshuk are stone figures that the Inuit use as hunting and navigational aids.

Mutiny!

The long search for the Northwest Passage is filled with cases of murder and **mutiny**. One of the most famous cases took place during Henry Hudson's fourth and final journey to search for the Northwest Passage. In 1610, Hudson and his crew left England and headed north. From the beginning of the journey, some members of the crew were unhappy. There were threats of mutiny. By November, the ship was frozen in ice. When the ship was finally free of the ice, Hudson decided to continue the expedition. The majority of the crew did not like this decision. They forced Hudson, his son, and several sick and loyal sailors into a small boat and then headed for home. Hudson and the others were never heard from again.

Fascinating Fact
Until the latter part of the eighteenth century, warfare between Europeans and the Inuit made southern Labrador and the Strait of Belle Isle—both located in what is now known as Canada—a dangerous place.

Finding the Northwest Passage

Early explorers quickly learned that the Northwest Passage would not be an easy trade route. However, eighteenth-century explorers continued to search the Arctic for a northern trade route. Explorers such as Samuel Hearne and Alexander Mackenzie searched for the passage on foot. They walked thousands of miles across the Canadian North. Some of the expeditions in the 1700s yielded useful and interesting information about the passage. However, wars between England and France in the early 1800s put the search for the Northwest Passage on hold.

By 1818, the wars had ended. England once again turned its attention to the Arctic. This time, the English were not searching for a road to riches. Instead, explorations were made in the interest of science. The people of England wanted the mysterious north filled in on their maps. Between 1818 and 1847, many sea and overland expeditions were launched to map the Arctic. The Franklin expedition was one of the most famous sea expeditions. John Franklin and a crew of 134 men left England in 1845. Sadly, the entire expedition disappeared in the North and was never seen again. In the following years, more than sixty-five expeditions were sent out to search for these missing men. On one of these expeditions in the 1850s, Robert McClure proved a Northwest Passage existed. He traveled from the Atlantic Ocean to the Pacific Ocean by ship and by dogsled.

The Mackenzie River in Canada is named after the explorer Alexander Mackenzie.

Scurvy

Early Arctic explorers did not have access to the fresh fruits and vegetables that contain vitamin C and other essential nutrients. As a result, many sailors contracted scurvy, a disease caused by a lack of vitamin C in the diet. In most cases, their skin turned black, their teeth fell out, and their gums bled. They suffered from ulcers and had difficulty breathing. A number of explorers died from scurvy. For many years, no one knew what caused scurvy. In 1747, a naval surgeon, James Lind, prescribed lemons and oranges as a cure for scurvy. In 1795, the British navy distributed lime juice during long sea voyages. This is the reason British sailors came to be known as *limeys*. Some Arctic explorers learned from the Inuit that whale blubber would prevent scurvy.

Dogsleds enabled explorers and hunters to enter hard-to-reach areas as well as carry large loads of supplies.

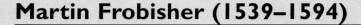

Martin Frobisher (1539–1594)

Martin Frobisher was one of the first explorers to search for the Northwest Passage. Frobisher was 14 years old when he went to sea for the first time. He became a well-known navigator and explorer. He was also a pirate who brought many treasures back to England and Queen Elizabeth I.

On June 7, 1576, Frobisher embarked on his first journey to the Arctic. With two ships and a crew of thirty-five men, he sailed north and landed near Resolution Island. He named this island "Queen Elizabeth's Forelande." He then sailed to the eastern tip of Hall Island and claimed the land in the queen's name. From there, he found a waterway he believed was the Northwest Passage. He named this waterway "Frobisher's Streights." Although he did not reach Asia, he returned to England with items from the North. One item was black rock, which he claimed contained gold.

In 1577, Frobisher was sent to the North for a second time. He returned from his second voyage with 200 tons (181 metric tonnes) of the black rock. He was sent back in 1578 to set up a colony and mine 2,000 tons (1,814 metric tonnes) of the black rock. Frobisher and his crew returned to England without finding any precious metals, such as gold. Soon after, it was discovered that the black rock he had found on his first voyage was worthless iron pyrite, or fool's gold. Despite this, Frobisher's journeys fueled further interest in exploring the North.

John Ross (1777–1856)

John Ross was born in Scotland in 1777. He learned his navigation skills on merchant ships. After **apprenticing**, he served with the British navy in the Napoleonic Wars (1803–1815). Following the end of the wars, the British Admiralty assigned Ross to lead an expedition into Davis Strait and Baffin Bay to search for the Northwest Passage. In April 1818, Ross left London with two ships. After reaching Davis Strait, he proceeded to Lancaster Sound. There, Ross became convinced he could see mountains in the distance and that the way was blocked. His crew thought he was wrong, but he decided to return to England. Ross's hasty decision tarnished his reputation. It was proven 1 year later that there were no mountains blocking Lancaster Sound. Ross had seen a **mirage**.

In 1829, Ross made another journey in search of the Northwest Passage. Ross sailed beyond Lancaster Sound and then south into Prince Regent Inlet. There, the ship got caught in ice. The crew was forced to spend the next 4 years in the Arctic. They were the first explorers to survive that long in the Arctic. During these years, Ross and his crew explored parts of the Arctic on foot. They collected scientific **specimens**. Ross's nephew, James Clark Ross, mapped the location of the **Magnetic North Pole**.

In 1833, Ross and his crew were rescued by a whaling ship and returned to England as heroes. Ross received thousands of letters congratulating him on his survival skills.

Sailors who ventured into the Arctic to find the Northwest Passage did not have it easy. They endured long voyages, often spending years at sea. These voyages were filled with danger, hardship, and hard work. Sailors toiled almost constantly while on board a ship. They performed their daily tasks in terrible winds and freezing temperatures. Sailors had many daily tasks. They watched for icebergs and land. They cleaned the decks. They cared for the sails. Their sleeping quarters were cramped and dirty. Their main food staples were beer, biscuits, and salted meat.

Fascinating Fact
Sailors did not own watches, so time was kept by ringing a bell.

Ice was the largest obstacle faced by early Arctic explorers. The sailors had a very short season in which they could actually sail on the Arctic waters. From late autumn to late spring, the northern waters were completely frozen. However, by July, the ice would begin to break apart into jagged **floes**. It was then that the sailors could continue their exploration. Still, the waters were never completely clear of

ice floes. This meant explorers had to ease their ships through very narrow channels created by the floes. Often, they had to tow their ships around the floes. Ships sometimes took days or even weeks to travel a few miles. Sailors had to do their best to fight their frustration.

Christopher Columbus was searching for a western water passage to Asia when he landed on the Caribbean Islands in 1492.

Christopher Columbus's Crew

Some people believe that Columbus's crew on the first voyage to the Americas were criminals. This is not true. They were nearly all experienced seamen. It is true that the Spanish monarchs offered freedom to any convict who signed up for the voyage. However, only four convicts accepted the offer. One convict had killed a man in a fight. The other three were his friends who had helped him escape from jail.

On the first voyage, the eighty-seven crewmen on the Niña, Pinta, and Santa Maria were paid between $12,509 and $25,018 U.S. in today's money. Masters and pilots were paid $50 to $200 U.S. per month. Able seamen were paid $50 to $100 U.S. per month. Ordinary seamen were paid $33 to $66 U.S. per month.

Sea ice in the Arctic has been melting rapidly over the past 3 decades.

The First European through the Northwest Passage

The Northwest Passage was proven to exist in the 1850s. It was another 50 years before a ship actually sailed through it. The man who sailed through the Northwest Passage was Roald Amundsen, an explorer from Norway. In 1903, Amundsen and six companions set sail on a small fishing boat called the *Gjoa*. By 1906, the crew had steered east to west through the passage. Amundsen kept an account of his journey. In it, he explains how his crew spotted a ship in the Pacific Ocean and knew they had successfully completed their journey.

The Pacific Ocean's name comes from the Spanish word *pacifico*, which means "peaceful."

At 8 a.m. my watch was finished and I turned in. When I had been asleep some time, I became conscious of a rushing to and fro on deck. Clearly there was something the matter, and I felt a bit annoyed that they should go on like that for the matter of a bear or a seal. It must be something of the kind, surely. But then Lieutenant Hansen came rushing down into the cabin and called out the ever memorable words: "Vessel in sight, sir!" He bolted again immediately and I was alone.

The North West Passage had been accomplished—my dream from childhood. This very moment it was fulfilled. I had a peculiar sensation in my throat; I was somewhat overworked and tired, and I suppose it was weakness on my part, but I could feel tears coming to my eyes. "Vessel in sight!" The words were magical.

Shortly after Roald Amundsen navigated the Northwest Passage, his ship was frozen into the ice. It remained in the ice all winter.

Modern Exploration

Since Roald Amundsen's successful journey through the Northwest Passage in the early 1900s, other explorers have continued to challenge the North's icy waters. In 1942, Royal Canadian Mounted Police Sergeant Henry Larsen became the second man to sail through the Northwest Passage. He and his crew sailed from Vancouver, British Columbia, to Halifax, Nova Scotia. It took Larsen and his crew 28 months to travel over the top of North America. They sailed in a **schooner** called the *St. Roch*. In 1944, Larsen turned the *St. Roch* around and completed the Northwest Passage from east to west in 86 days.

Both Amundsen and Larsen used relatively small vessels to navigate the Northwest Passage. However, later twentieth-century explorers began to tackle the passage in more powerful ships called icebreakers. In 1954, a 6,500-ton (5,900-metric tonne) Canadian icebreaker called the *Labrador* plowed through the passage in only 68 days. Over the next few years, other icebreakers continued to chart new northern routes. In 1969, a group of oil companies spent $40 million to equip an enormous oil tanker called the *Manhattan* with a powerful engine and a special ice-breaking bow. It was seventeen times larger than any ship to sail through the passage. The enormous oil tanker made the trip in record time. However, it suffered serious damage. Once again, plans to use the passage for profit were abandoned.

Fascinating Fact
In 1960, the United States Navy nuclear submarine *Sea Dragon* pioneered another northwest passage by traveling under the polar ice.

Oil companies wanted to use the Northwest Passage to transport oil from Alaska to Philadelphia.

The Icebreaker

Icebreakers are heavy ships designed to break the thick ice in Arctic and Antarctic waters. Modern icebreakers are made of steel. They have a double hull and a rounded bow. The rounded bow enables an icebreaker to rise on top of the ice. This allows the ship's weight to break through ice much like a sledgehammer breaks through cement. Russian and American icebreakers are able to break through ice 6 to 7 feet (1.8–2.1 m) thick.

Icebreakers are very expensive to build and operate. They are also uncomfortable to ride in—breaking through the ice causes constant vibration and noise. Still, these powerful boats have made it possible to sail through polar waters with greater ease and fewer tragedies.

Icebreakers shoot hot water at Arctic ice through jets located just below the water line.

Lasting Effects

For centuries, the long, difficult search for the Northwest Passage was a popular subject among Europeans. The public listened to the tales of explorers who had braved the North and survived. Many explorers wrote books about their Arctic adventures. Early artists created paintings and drawings of the Arctic based on explorers' stories. Today, the history and present state of the Northwest Passage fascinate many people. Songs, books, and films about the passage are still produced. Also, new types of exploration are being conducted in the Arctic. For example, the Mars Society is a group preparing people to travel to Mars. This group is conducting experiments and testing equipment on Devon Island in the Canadian Arctic. Devon Island is one of the most Mars-like environments on Earth.

Fascinating Fact
Since 1906, only 60 ships have traveled the entire length of the Northwest Passage.

The Northwest Passage is not considered a good shipping route because of ice. However, many scientists claim that the Arctic **icecap** is slowly melting. According to these scientists, global warming has already begun to slowly melt the icecap over the North. It is possible that in just a few decades global warming will have melted enough of the ice to open the Northwest Passage for shipping, tourism, and fishing, at least for part of the year. Such a possibility would have been a dream come true 400 years ago.

Devon Island is located in Nunavut. It is the largest uninhabited island in the world.

Arctic Sovereignty

The northern lands around the Northwest Passage belong to Canada. Canadian officials consider the waters of the passage internal waters. This means they believe that non-Canadian vessels must request permission to pass. However, the United States and other countries do not accept Canada's claim to **sovereignty** over the waters of the Northwest Passage. In 1969 and 1985, the United States sent oil tankers into Canada's Arctic without permission. The United States argued that it had a right to send the tankers because Arctic waters are not internationally recognized as belonging to Canada. In 1988, Canada and the United States reached an agreement that allowed U.S. icebreakers access to Arctic waters on a case-by-case basis.

Submarines allow scientists to explore areas that are hard to reach in the Northwest Passage.

Northwest Passage Time Line

1497 to 1498
John Cabot claims Newfoundland for England.

1534 to 1542
French explorer Jacques Cartier surveys the coast of Canada and the St. Lawrence River and searches for the Northwest Passage.

1576 to 1578
Martin Frobisher makes three voyages to the North and reaches Baffin Island and Frobisher Bay.

1585 to 1587
John Davis commands three voyages in an attempt to find the Northwest Passage. He makes a correct guess about the location of the entrance to the passage.

1609 to 1611
Henry Hudson explores North America's east coast and sails on the river and bay that now bear his name.

1818 to 1833
John Ross embarks on three expeditions to the Arctic. On the second expedition, Ross and his men are trapped in the Arctic for 4 years.

1845
John Franklin leads an expedition by sea in search of the Northwest Passage. Officers and crew are trapped by ice off King William Island. The entire crew is dead by 1848.

1850 to 1854
Robert McClure penetrates the Pacific entrance to the Northwest Passage and completes the passage partly by ship and partly by dogsled.

1903 to 1906
Roald Amundsen successfully navigates the Northwest Passage by ship.

1942
Sergeant Henry Larsen becomes the second man to sail through the Northwest Passage. He is the first to travel from west to east.

1944
Sergeant Henry Larsen completes the Northwest Passage from east to west in a single season.

1969
The oil tanker *Manhattan* sails the Northwest Passage in less than a month.

Activity:
Tales from the Arctic

The four-century search for the Northwest Passage was filled with excitement, adventure, and tragedy. Many explorers were admired and celebrated for the expeditions they led into the Far North. Others were shamed for their failures. Still others died on their quests. Below are the names of ten men who devoted much of their lives to finding the Northwest Passage. Choose one explorer, and research his journey to the Arctic. Once you have learned all about his northern voyage(s), imagine you are one of the crew members on the expedition. Write a long journal entry or letter to a loved one that describes the explorer and the journey he is leading.

Martin Frobisher	**John Ross**
John Davis	**William Parry**
William Baffin	**John Franklin**
Robert Bylot	**Robert McClure**
Henry Hudson	**Roald Amundsen**

Quiz

1. Who was the first explorer to complete the Northwest Passage?

2. What disease plagued many sailors during their quest to find the Northwest Passage?

3. Which Arctic explorer saw mountains blocking a passage through Lancaster Sound?

4. Name two navigational instruments used by sailors.

5. Whose lost expedition caused explorers after him to chart much of the unknown Arctic?

6. Why was the Northwest Passage important?

7. Who first explored North America's Arctic regions?

8. Who found fool's gold while searching for the Northwest Passage?

9. What is the biggest obstacle in Arctic waters?

10. Name the first boat to navigate through the Northwest Passage.

Answers on page 32.

Further Research

Web sites

www.allthingsarctic.com
This site contains profiles of several important Arctic explorers as well as fascinating facts about the Arctic and the search for the Northwest Passage.

www.nlc-bnc.ca/2/24/index-e.html
This site presents a history of the search for the Northwest Passage century by century.

Books

Blashfield, Jean F. *Cartier: Jacques Cartier in Search of the Northwest Passage*. Minneapolis: Compass Point Books, 2002.

Warrick, Karen Clemens. *The Perilous Search for the Fabled Northwest Passage in American History*. Berkeley Heights, NJ: Enslow, 2004.

Glossary

altitude: the height of something above a particular specified level, especially above sea level or Earth's surface

apprenticing: learning a trade or skill

bow: the forward part of a ship

commandeer: to seize another's property for public or military use

expeditions: journeys or voyages that are made for a specific purpose, such as exploration

floes: sheets of floating ice

global warming: an increase in Earth's atmospheric temperature, causing changes in the climate and environment

hulls: the bodies or frames of ships

icecap: a thick cover of ice over an area

labyrinth: a maze of paths or passages

Magnetic North Pole: the spot on Earth to which the north moves a little bit each year

mirage: a misleading appearance of something in the distance; an illusion

mutiny: a rebellion against legal authority, especially by soldiers or sailors refusing to obey orders and, often, attacking their officers

navigation: the science of getting ships, aircraft, or spacecraft from place to place

nomadic: moving from place to place, with no permanent home

overland: proceeding over or across land

schooner: a fast sailing ship with at least two masts and with its sails parallel to the length of the ship rather than across it

sheathed: covered

sophisticated: complicated or complex

sovereignty: having power or authority over a region

specimens: typical examples of animals, plants, and minerals

Index

Answers to Quiz on Page 30
1. Robert McClure **2.** scurvy **3.** John Ross **4.** the cross-staff and the back-staff **5.** John Franklin **6.** The Northwest Passage offered an alternate trade route to Asia and the riches of Cathay. **7.** the Inuit **8.** Martin Frobisher **9.** ice **10.** the *Gjoa*